The Great Gatsby Study Guide 2020

CRACK THE COMPARATIVE #1

Amy Farrell

SCENE BY SCENE
WICKLOW, IRELAND

Copyright © 2019 by Scene by Scene.

Without limiting the rights under copyright, this book is sold subject to the condition that it shall not, by way of trade or otherwise be lent, resold, hired out, reproduced, stored on or introduced into a retrieval system, or transmitted, in any form or by any means (electronic, mechanical, photocopying, recording or otherwise), or otherwise circulated, without the publisher's prior consent, in any form other than that in which it is published and without a similar condition, including this condition, being imposed on the subsequent publisher.

All rights reserved. No part of this publication may be recorded or transmitted in any form or by any means electronic, mechanical, photocopying, recording or otherwise without the proper consent of the publisher.

The publisher reserves the right to change, without notice, at any time, the specification of this product, whether by change of materials, colours, format, text revision or any other characteristic.

Scene by Scene
Wicklow, Ireland.
www.scenebyscene.ie

The Great Gatsby Study Guide 2020 by Amy Farrell.
ISBN 978-1-910949-78-8

Cover Image © Etraveler | Dreamstime.com

Contents

About This Book	1
Understanding the Mode - Cultural Context/Social Setting	2
Notes on Cultural Context/Social Setting	4
Cultural Context/Social Setting - Key Moments	6
Visiting Daisy and Tom Buchanan in East Egg	6
Nick's First Party at Gatsby's	7
Lunch in the City	8
Gatsby Meets Daisy and Shows Her Around His Home	9
The Plaza Hotel	10
After Gatsby's Death	11
Understanding the Mode - Literary Genre	13
Notes on Literary Genre	15
Literary Genre Key Moments	18
The Novel's Opening	18
Party in the City	19
Nick's First Party at Gatsby's	20
Car Accident	20
Gatsby's Death	22
The Ending	23
Understanding the Mode - Theme/Issue – Relationships	24
Notes on Theme/Issue - Relationships	26
Theme/Issue - Relationships Key Moments	28
Nick Visits Daisy and Tom	28
Party in the City	29
Gatsby is Reunited with Daisy	30
Confrontation at the Plaza Hotel	30
Post Accident	31

Nick's Loyalty to Gatsby After His Death	32
Understanding the Mode - Hero, Heroine, Villain (Ordinary Level)	33
Notes on Hero, Heroine, Villain (Ordinary Level)	34
Hero, Heroine, Villain Key Moments	36
Gatsby's Reputation	36
Lunch in the City with Nick	36
Meeting Daisy	37
Tom Ends Gatsby's Affair with Daisy	38
Attempting to Protect Daisy After the Accident	39
Post Death Version of Gatsby	39

About This Book

This book is a study guide for Leaving Certificate English students sitting their exam in 2020. It provides notes for the Comparative Study of *The Great Gatsby* by F. Scott Fitzgerald.

There are notes and analysis of key moments for Cultural Context/Social Setting, Literary Genre, Theme/Issue (Relationships) and Hero, Heroine, Villain.

I have selected key moments to analyse for each comparative study mode. However, my choices are not definitive - any moment can be considered and explored for any mode. Feel free to consider other moments to add to your analysis for the comparative study.

The Great Gatsby by F. Scott Fitzgerald

The Great Gatsby is a story of hollow wealth and the illusion of glamour, revolving around the narrator's enigmatic neighbour, Jay Gatsby.

Understanding the Mode
Cultural Context/Social Setting

Cultural Context/Social Setting refers to the world of the text. Think about social norms, beliefs, values and attitudes.

Consider the following questions to help you understand the Cultural Context/Social Setting of *The Great Gatsby*.

- What time and place is the story set in?

- What are the rules that characters live by?

- What guides characters' behaviour?

- What do characters fear?

- What do characters believe in – religion, power, love, family, wealth?

- What do characters prioritise – family, money, reputation?

- Who holds the power in this world?
  Who is powerless?

- How are the vulnerable members of society treated in this world?
  Are they protected or persecuted?

- Is this a supportive, loving world?

- Is this a harsh, threatening world?

- How does this world impact on characters' lives and relationships?

- How free are characters in this world?

- How controlled are characters in this world?
  Who controls them?
  Who has the power?
  Why do they have this power?
  Why are they obeyed/why are rules followed?

- What strikes you about the society of the text?

- What is the world of this text like?

- What is it like to live here?

Notes on Cultural Context/Social Setting

The novel is set in **the world of the rich elite of 1920s New York**. Jay Gatsby, the narrator's mysterious, charasmatic neighbour, throws **splendid, lavish parties** all summer long. **This is a world full of the glamour of wealth.**

Social standing and reputation are very significant in this world. Guests swarm uninvited to Gatsby's lavish parties all summer where they trade **gossip and rumours** about him. These whispers are sensational stories about Gatsby: that he killed a man, that he was a German spy during the war, that he was in the American army. There is mystery and intrigue surrounding Gatsby that makes him exciting to these **rich, idle party-goers**. They come to these parties for **fun and excitement**, enjoying the **dancing and drinking**.

When Gatsby meets Daisy, he is keen for her to see his fine clothes, beautiful home and grounds. **This is a materialistic world, where wealth and luxury impress.**

In this world, **infidelity appears to be the norm**. Daisy and Tom have affairs outside their marriage, as does Tom's lover, Myrtle, while Gatsby pursues Daisy, knowing that she is married. **Being married does not deter these relationships in this society.**

However, **despite their extramarital affairs, characters appear to be romantic and devoted to their pursuit of love**. Gatsby chose his home to be across the water from Daisy, a very romantic idea. He has built his life around reconnecting with her and being in love with her, despite the fact that she is now married.

Tom, Daisy's husband, has a good relationship with her, despite his affairs. When Gatsby announces that Daisy never loved Tom, Tom is quick to defend his marriage, saying that while he might go on a spree and make a fool of himself, he loves Daisy all the while and always comes back to her. It appears that **being faithful is not a prerequisite of being in love** here.

Characters in this world have **little to do with work**, rather they are **absorbed in the business of enjoying themselves and attending parties**.

Similarly, Daisy does not trouble herself with the care of her daughter, these **rich characters can afford to employ someone to mind their children while they enjoy themselves**.

There is a hidden, darker side to the world of the novel. There is a **dangerous, criminal side to Gatsby's life, hidden from view**. Gatsby is somehow involved in crime, when he dies in violent circumstances his friends and acquaintances evaporate, not wanting to be associated with him.

This suggests **illegal activity**, but also **a cold world, where friendship counts for little**. Following Gatsby's death, his friends and acquaintances vanish, with virtually nobody willing to acknowledge that they knew him. His friend, Meyer Wolfshiem, refuses to attend his funeral, not wanting to get mixed up in it, now that Gatsby has been killed. Gatsby's friends have vanished, suggesting that he was used for his lavish parties, and is **easily forgotten now that scandal is attached to his name**.

Reputation is more important than friendship or loyalty, and so Gatsby is quickly disowned. The speed with which Gatsby's circle disown him shows how shallow and superficial these connections were. **What matters to these people is not friendship, but reputation**, and nobody wants to be linked to Gatsby anymore.

In this world Gatsby was able to invent himself and forget

his lowly beginnings as Jimmy Gatz. However, while money can earn him a new identity and a glamorous lifestyle, it cannot make certain his place in the world. Now that he has died in sensational circumstances he is quickly discarded and forgotten.

It is worth noting that **this is not a world where truth or justice triumphs**. Daisy and Tom leave town after Myrtle's death, and so Daisy gets off scot-free, never having to answer for her crime. This shows **the injustice of the class system in this world, where the rich can easily protect themselves and do as they please.**

This was also true for Gatsby, who during his life enjoyed a splendid lifestyle and immense popularity, despite his criminal activities. This is a world of wealth and glamour, a place of excitement and riches, but it is also a cold, calculating world, as Gatsby's death and disappearing friends illustrate.

Gatsby's celebrity and popularity do not last. It is an illusion, brief and fleeting, in this society of the rich and bored who want to be entertained. He is quickly forgotten in this formal world that does not wish to dwell on the darker side of life.

Cultural Context/Social Setting Key Moments

Visiting Daisy and Tom Buchanan in East Egg

Nick goes to visit Tom and Daisy in their **mansion in fashionable East**

Egg, describing them as "**two old friends whom I scarcely knew at all**". Nick describes their **extravagant home** and **leisurely lifestyle**, giving the reader an insight into their wealthy lives. Tom is in his riding clothes, Daisy and her friend laze on a huge couch while they **chat and drink cocktails** with Nick.

Nick notes the **relaxed pace of the evening**, feeling how different it is to the rushed evenings back West, with talk of crops.

Tom talks about the dominance of the white race, and the need to preserve it, which Daisy seems to find amusing.

Tom goes to a take a phonecall, and Daisy goes indoors. Jordan Baker, Daisy's friend, tries to listen to what is being said. She tells Nick that **Tom has a woman in New York, something she thought everyone knew. Tom's affair is public knowledge.**

When Daisy and Tom return to the table, they all **do their best to pretend that nothing of note has occured**, suggesting a **polite, restrained society that avoids confrontation.**

After Jordan goes to bed, Tom remarks that she is a nice girl, and that her family should not let her run around the country the way they do, showing that he **disapproves of her freedom.**

Before he leaves, Tom and Daisy ask Nick about a rumour they heard that he was engaged. He denies it, telling the reader that he came East in part because of this **gossip.**

Nick's First Party at Gatsby's

Nick describes **the extravagance and expense of Gatsby's parties** and the fleet of staff he hires to maintain his mansion and **entertain his guests**. His house is always full of life and excitement, with guests arriving at all hours of the day and night.

The catering staff, orchestra and bar all show **Gatsby's wealth** and give us a picture of the **glamorous lifestyle lived by the rich elite of 1920s New York**.

Nick is invited to his first party by Gatsby's chauffeur, but many of the **guests turn up without an invitation**. Gatsby's is a destination for partying into the night for the rich and well connected.

His mansion is a magical, luxurious place, full of romance and mystery, "In his blue gardens men and girls came and went like moths among the whisperings and the champagne and the stars."

Guests exchange **stories and rumours** about their host as they drink and eat well into the night. Nick chats to a man about the war before the man reveals, to Nick's surprise, that he is Gatsby. He is a mysterious and enigmatic host.

Lunch in the City

Gatsby arrives one morning to take Nick to lunch. On the drive, he asks Nick his opinion of him, suggesting that **Gatsby is concerned about his reputation and the opinion others hold him in**. Gatsby says he will tell Nick something of his life, so that he does not get the wrong idea from all the stories he hears. Gatsby is aware of the **rumours and gossip** about him, and seeks to repair Nick's opinion of him.

Nick does not entirely believe Gatsby's version of events, but is convinced when Gatsby produces an army medal and a photograph from Oxford.

Gatsby explains that he has a favour to ask of Nick, and wants him to know something about him first. This gives the impression of a **formal society, where matters are carefully weighed and measured** rather than being rushed into.

As they carry on, Gatsby is stopped by a motorcycle policeman, who excuses himself when he realises that Gatsby has a connection to the commissioner. **Gatsby is well connected with very influential people.**

They meet Gatsby's friend, Mr Wolfshiem, for lunch, who mistakenly asks Nick if he is looking for a business connection. When he leaves, Gatsby tells Nick that Wolfshiem is a gambler, and that he fixed the World Series in 1919 but has eluded jail. **This meeting with Wolfshiem gives an insight into the shady workings of Gatsby's business connections.**

Gatsby Meets Daisy and Shows Her Around His Home

Jordan speaks to Nick on Gatsby's behalf regarding his desire to meet Daisy. This is a **rather formal** arrangement, with Gatsby needing time to prepare for Daisy's visit. He awkwardly **offers Nick some work of a dubious nature**, which Nick turns down. It seems that Gatsby is involved in some **shady business affairs**.

When Nick contacts Daisy the next day and invites her to tea, he tells her **not to bring her husband**. She is **happy to visit without him**, suggesting that they lead very independent lives.

Gatsby prepares for Daisy's visit by ordering flowers, cutting the grass and dressing in a resplendent suit. When she arrives, Nick tells her to send her chauffeur away for an hour, ensuring **privacy**.

Gatsby is **strained and nervous** meeting Daisy, and they are both **awkward and ill at ease** at first. Gatsby tells Nick he has made a terrible mistake, and Nick tells him that he is just embarrassed.

Once Gatsby and Daisy are reacquainted, **Gatsby is eager for her to see his house**, which she admires and compliments. Gatsby takes Daisy from room to room, revelling in her **appreciation of his home and possessions**, showing **the value of materialistic wealth** in this world. **Daisy cries when she sees his beautiful shirts, showing the superficiality of their world of wealth and riches.**

The Plaza Hotel

At a loss for what to do, Daisy suggests that they go to town. They are rich and idle, looking for something to occupy them. Theirs is a privileged world of wealth and comfort.

As they wait for the women to get ready, **Gatsby tells Nick that he cannot say anything to Tom about him and Daisy in Tom's house.** This shows a **formal politeness and restraint** on Gatsby's part.

They stop for gas on the way and Wilson tells Tom that he and his wife (Myrtle, Tom's girlfriend), are moving West, whether she wants to or not. Wilson's solution to realising that there is something going on with his wife is to **force her to move away. As her husband, he will make this choice for them both.**

Tom, Daisy, Nick and Jordan engage the parlour of a suite in the Plaza Hotel, which shows their **wealth and the rich lifestyle** they enjoy. There is a certain **aimlessness** in their **world of luxury and privilege.**

Tom asks Gatsby what kind of a row he is trying to cause in his house, and Daisy tries to quiet him, telling him to have some self-control. **Outbursts like this are not the norm** in this world.

Gatsby tells Tom that Daisy never loved him, only ever loving Gatsby. This shows the **romantic, idealistic side of this world**, with Gatsby desperately believing that his love is unique and untouchable. Tom puts Daisy's actions down to foolishness rather than lack of love. He insists that Daisy loves him, and he her.

Tom admits to going on sprees and making a fool of himself, but says he always comes back, and loves her all the while. **Tom clearly takes his marriage seriously, and feels committed to Daisy, but does not view being faithful as part of that commitment.**

Tom is determined that Daisy does not leave him, and he reveals Gatsby as a "common swindler". **Tom shreds Gatsby's reputation**, telling the others about his **shady business ventures**. Gatsby tries to deny these allegations and defend his name to Daisy, but their bond has been broken.

Daisy is no longer interested in Gatsby, now that she knows of his illegal activities. **His reputation is undone, and so too is Daisy's romantic interest in him, showing the value of reputation in this society.**

After Gatsby's Death

Gatsby's murder is a scandal, his house is overrun with police, photographers and newspaper men. Nick mentions nightmare reports in the news, showing how **sensational** the story is.

Nick finds that **Gatsby's friends and acquaintances have vanished**. Nobody is interested in looking after Gatsby's affairs. **He has no wealthy lineage, no family to step in. In this world of Old Money, he is a

nobody once more.

Nick tries to reach Daisy, but she and Tom have left town. **Daisy has escaped, and will not have to face court for accidentally killing Myrtle Wilson. Her wealth protects her**, allowing her to slip away. In this society, rules do not apply to the wealthy.

Wolfshiem, Gatsby's friend and business connection, avoids Gatsby's funeral, not wanting to "get mixed up in this thing now." **Friendship counts for nothing, trumped by the importance of preserving one's reputation.**

The **darker side of this world** is glimpsed when Nick receives a phonecall from Chicago, telling him that young Parke's in trouble, that he was picked up when he handed the bonds over the counter. Although the exact situation is unclear, it seems that **Gatsby was involved in crime. His splendid, extravagant lifestyle was funded by his illegal business dealings.** When Nick tells the caller that Gatsby is dead, the connection is broken, leaving Nick with unanswered questions about Gatsby. We are left to wonder whether it is possible to really know him in this **superficial world where characters can invent themselves.**

The **superficiality of this world** is highlighted when Gatsby's father, Mr Gatz, speaks of his son Jimmy. By using a different name, it is almost as if he speaks of a different person. It shows how little Nick really knew of Gatsby.

The **coldness and heartlessness of this society** is clear when Klipspringer phones seeking the return of a pair of shoes. He says he **cannot attend Gatsby's funeral, as he is going to a picnic instead.** Gatsby's funeral does not impact on the **purposefully carefree lifestyle of the rich and glamorous. Few mourners attend the funeral, despite the** hundreds that flocked to his lavish parties all summer long. In this world, Gatsby, it seems, is easily forgotten.

Understanding the Mode
Literary Genre

Literary Genre focuses on the ways that texts tell their stories. When analysing Literary Genre, consider the choices the author makes in telling their story this way, and how this impacts on the reader's experience of the story. Think about aspects of narration such as the manner and style of narration, characterisation, setting, tension, literary techniques, etc.

Consider these questions when thinking about Literary Genre.

- How is this story told? (Who tells it? Where and when is it told? How is it structured? What does this add?)

- Why is the story told in this way?

- How does setting add to the story?

- Who is the main character (protagonist)? Do you like them? Why/why not?

- What are the protagonist's main characteristics? Are they an appealing character? Why/why not?

- How does this character change and develop during the course of the story? (character's arc) What causes these changes? Can you plot/chart these changes and developments?

- How does this character interact with other characters? How does this add to the story?

- How are atmosphere and mood created? How do they add to the story?

- Is symbolism used to add to the storytelling?

- How do you respond to the narrative voice?

- Is this an exciting/engaging story? Why/why not?

- Does the author make good use of conflict/tension/suspense?

- What are your favourite moments in the story? What makes these moments stand out for you?

- How does this story make you feel? How does it cause you to feel this way?

- Is there just one plot or many plots? How do these relate to one another?

- What are the major tensions in the text? Are they resolved or not?

- Is this way of telling the story successful and enjoyable?

- Is the story humorous or tragic, romantic or realistic?

- To what genre does it belong?
  Is it Romance, Thriller, Social Realism, Saga, Historical, Fantasy, Science Fiction, Satire?

Notes on Literary Genre

This novel is told from the **point of view of Nick Carraway, Gatsby's neighbour**. The **first person perspective** means that we follow Nick's point of view, and learn information and details as he does, **he is our filter** for the story.

The **character** of Jay **Gatsby, Nick's rich, enigmatic neighbour** adds **excitement and mystery** to the text. Nick is drawn to learning more of Gatsby, and following his death, finds himself as Gatsby's sole friend. He attempts to find out more about the man, to unravel his life and mysterious persona, which adds drama and excitement to the story.

Gatsby himself is an **intriguing, likeable character**. His **wealth** and lavish parties **invite the reader's curiosity**, as does his **love affair** with Daisy, and his **shady background** that we discover after his death. **This intrigue surrounding Gatsby makes the narrative compelling.**

There is a **surreal atmosphere to much of the novel, not everything is as it seems. Gatsby has created his identity**, having lowly beginnings as James Gatz, until reinventing himself at seventeen.

He also met Daisy before going overseas with the army, he has **multiple identites and personas** that **add a mysterious quality to both his** character and the story itself.

Coupled with this are **his extravagant lifestyle and over the top, glamorous parties, which also add an air of unreality to the story.** The beautiful imagery and rich description add to the sense of the almost surreal glamour and luxury of this world.

There is **conflict and tension** in **Gatsby's affair with Daisy**, and Tom's realisation of it, which culminates in the stiflingly hot hotel room where Tom exposes Gatsby as a bootlegger, deflating his dream of a future with Daisy. This is an exciting **plot development**.

Following this episode, the **tension is further increased** when we learn how Myrtle has been killed by a car speeding from New York, the car that the reader knows contains Gatsby and Daisy. Wilson knows this yellow car, having seen Tom in it before, **adding to the tension**.

Myrtle's accidental death sets in motion the events that will lead to Gatsby's murder and Nick's attempts to find Gatsby's friends and acquaintances. **Gatsby's conviction that Daisy will leave Tom, the description of Wilson searching to find the driver of the car, and Nick's description of Gatsby's final afternoon, add to the excitement of this sequence**. It is almost **cinematic** as the reader imagines these events unfolding.

Gatsby is shot in his pool, a **dramatic and shocking** moment in the story, resulting from Wilson's belief that Gatsby has killed his wife. **Gatsby's death is a climactic moment in the novel**, a high point that follows quickly after Myrtle's accidental death. The **pacing** here keeps the reader gripped in the story, as these events are both shocking and exciting.

There is **great emotional weight in the description of Gatsby's death**. He has tried to protect Daisy from Tom, and from being discovered as the driver of the car that struck Myrtle, which shows the caring side of his **character**. His **back story** about Daisy, which immediately precedes his death, also **reinforces the impression of him as a hopeful, loving man**. In fact, the last thing he speaks to Nick about is his hope that Daisy will call. **At this point in the story, the reader likes Gatsby, and admires his positive outlook and belief in love. This makes his death all the more affecting and shocking for the reader, when he dies for something he did not do**. Though by no means perfect, Gatsby is innocent in the matter of Myrtle's accident, which adds to the reader's sense of shock and outrage on reading of his murder, making this an **emotional high point** in the text.

The novel's final chapter details Nick's attempts to track down friends and acquaintances of Gatsby's following his untimely death. However, he runs into one dead end after another, as nobody wants to be associated with Gatsby anymore.

Nick's attempts to put Gatsby's affairs in order are a testament to friendship, and to Nick's loyalty to Gatsby. However, **he fails to truly resolve the question of who Gatsby really is,** and **the story ends with the man's mystery and enigmatic charm intact.**

There is also the sense that Gatsby has been cheated somehow, that his successful life was all an illusion.

The reader feels that we have witnessed a glimpse of this world of luxury and extravagance, just as Nick has. Without Gatsby, he chooses to leave West Egg, just as the reader must do.

Literary Genre Key Moments

The Novel's Opening

The author builds reader anticipation and excitement in the way he introduces Gatsby, the novel's protagonist. He **describes Gatsby as an exception**, having "something gorgeous about him", and says it is unlikely that he will meet such a person again.

The writer then changes the **pace**, speaking of his own background, his move to New York, and a meeting with his cousin Daisy and her husband Tom. At this stage, little does the reader realise how instrumental Daisy and Tom will be in the story. **Key characters are carefully introduced as the novel's setting is built and developed**. It is only at the end of the first chapter that the narrator, Nick, first catches sight of Gatsby stargazing on his lawn. Nick is about to call out to him, when he notices Gatsby trembling as he looks across the water to a light on a far away dock. When Nick glances back, Gatsby has vanished.

In this description, Fitzgerald establishes Gatsby as a romantic, mysterious character, at once nearby and distant. This is **the foundation for Gatsby's illusive character** that will be built on over the course of the novel. Interestingly, **Gatsby's actions as he gazes across the water are significant**. We will learn that he looks over towards Daisy's home, longing to be with her. Just as Nick's afternoon with Daisy and Tom may have appeared insignificant at first, so too will this detail gain significance as the story progresses. The author is **carefully building these details to lay greater meaning over them later on**.

Party in the City

Nick meets Tom's mistress and spends an afternoon with them in New York. This episode **develops the reader's understanding of the characters and setting**, and **introduces conflict** into the storyline.

Myrtle, Tom's woman, is described as a "thickish figure", "faintly stout" with "no facet or gleam of beauty" to her face. Fitzgerald **catches the reader off guard, she is not described as being beautiful**, we must look beyond the obvious and pay attention to learn more of her affair with Tom.

A **surreal, dreamlike quality** is added to this moment by the spontaneous purchase of a dog on the way to the apartment. This ill-advised purchase is not thought out, giving an insight into Myrtle and Tom's personalities and relationship, but also adding an **unreal, incredible feeling** to this section.

This is compounded by Nick saying that he was drunk on this occasion, adding a **dim, hazy cast to the events of the afternoon**. In this way, the writer creates this **surreal scene** for the reader.

Tom's infidelity introduces friction and conflict to the plot. He is openly unfaithful, it is well-known, and his behaviour here adds to our understanding of his **character**. Tom is someone who does as he chooses. His lack of commitment to Daisy, and his selfish arrogance, establishes him as a **negative character** in the story, something that is confirmed when he lashes out at Myrtle, breaking her nose.

Nick's First Party at Gatsby's

Nick precedes his account of his first party at Gatsby's with a **description of the luxury and lavish extravagance that Gatsby's guests enjoy.** He describes these guests almost as exotic creatures, "In his blue gardens men and girls came and went like moths among the whisperings and the champagne and the stars." The writer creates **a sense of romance, glamour and mystery,** which **builds reader curiosity and anticipation. Through Nick, the reader will also experience these splendid parties and taste this lifestyle.**

A chauffeur invites Nick to the party, who dresses for the occasion, adding to the **formality and ceremony** of the event.

Few of the guests know much of Gatsby and **rumours abound**, adding to the **mystery and intrigue** of the man. Nick and Jordan happen upon a guest in the library who is amazed that Gatsby's books are real. His expectation that they were fake feeds into the **theme of superficiality and pretence** that runs through the story, while adding to the **intrigue of Gatsby's character,** about whom we know so little. Indeed, Nick is chatting with Gatsby before he ever realises who he is speaking to.

In this way, Nick's experience at his first party in Gatsby's **highlights the glamour and luxury of the time,** while **developing the reader's sense of Gatsby as an enigmatic, mysterious character.**

Car Accident

Myrtle's accidental death is a dramatic high point in the text. It occurs directly after the showdown in the Plaza Hotel, where Tom confronts

Gatsby about his affair with Daisy.

The **pacing** here is very effective, as the crash swiftly follows the emotional argument between Tom and Gatsby in the hotel room, and Daisy's choosing of her husband over Gatsby once he is revealed as a bootlegger and shady business man.

The **reader is still processing this intense scene when we learn of Myrtle's death**. The **fast paced action** adds to the **excitement**.

Fitzgerald signals Myrtle's approaching death by saying "we drove on toward death through the cooling twilight", a line full of **romantic mystery and intrigue.**

The author adopts the **perspective** of Michaelis, Wilson's neighbour, as he begins to recount the details of the accident, building **tension** as the story develops. Wilson tells his neighbour that he has his wife locked up, increasing the tension through this **conflict**.

Michaelis heard Mrs Wilson's voice raised in argument before she ran out in front of the 'death car'. The **domestic drama** of Wilson and Myrtle is well-known to the reader, this story is tied to Tom, and so is an exciting **plot development**.

What makes this moment so **tense**, is that Myrtle was struck by a yellow car coming from New York, a car the reader knows contains Gatsby and Daisy. The reader is on the inside track, with more knowledge than characters at the scene.

The **tension in the aftermath of this shocking revelation is maintained** as Tom tries to prevent Wilson from saying too much in front of the police. Tom tells Wilson to pull himself together and asserts that the yellow car is not his before leaving. In this way the **tension is sustained,** the matter of Myrtle's killing has yet to be reckoned. The reader, like Tom and Nick, is one step ahead of the police, we know what has taken place, and that trouble is coming for Gatsby. His splendid car, a symbol of his wealth and style, will now link him to Myrtle's sensational death.

Gatsby's Death

The author **describes the build-up to Gatsby's death**, creating **tension** and **cinematically setting the scene by describing Wilson's actions and the timeframe involved in minute detail**. The reader learns that by the time he was in West Egg, Wilson was asking for Gatsby's house by name. He has found the owner of the yellow car and set himself on a deadly, unalterable course.

The author builds the atmosphere as Nick imagines Gatsby's last moments in his pool, reflecting on how his world has changed. Aspects of the scene are described as "unfamiliar", "frightening", "grotesque" and "raw" as Nick imagines the world through Gatsby's eyes. **The reader is being prepared for an unnatural, shocking occurrence**. The spell of Gatsby's charmed existence is about to be destroyed.

Wilson's killing of Gatsby is relayed indirectly to the reader. Nick **charts the events leading to the discovery of Gatsby's body**: the chauffeur heard shots, he, the butler, the gardener and Nick hurried to Gatsby's pool. **Gatsby's body is not described**, the only reference to violence is a "thin red circle in the water".

Nick tells us "the gardener saw Wilson's body a little way off in the grass, and the holocaust was complete." Nick describes the chain of events leading up to this murder-suicide, but omits the gruesome reality of the scene. We are spared a description of the dead bodies. **It is up to the reader to piece together the details and imagine exactly what has taken place.**

Gatsby's death is a shocking occurrence that releases tension and impacts emotionally on the reader. In this moment we are forced to consider the injustice of Gatsby's death, and the sad way things have turned out for him. Nick describes the strangeness and harshness of the world just before Gatsby's murder. This idea will be developed as **Gatsby's world begins to unravel and fall asunder** following his violent death.

The Ending

The final stages of the novel are filled with **Nick's attempts to seek a resolution to what has happened**, and put Gatsby to rest in a fitting way. Like Nick, whose **perspective** we share, the reader has many unanswered questions. However, **answers about Gatsby are hard to find**. Now that he has died in sensational circumstances, Gatsby's friends vanish, no-one wants to be linked to this man who they adored in life.

Nick fails to rouse friends for Gatsby after his death, leaving the reader with a **hollow sense of dissatisfaction**. This is compounded by the way that Daisy and Tom escape back to their life of privilege while Gatsby pays for Myrtle's death with his life. This adds to our impression of the **society and setting** of this world. In this place, those from rich, wealthy families can do as they choose, without consequence.

The **question of identity** is revisited as Nick attempts to discover who the true Gatsby was. It seems he was many men. Nick fields a call from Chicago about young Parke being in trouble. This call suggests criminality and shady business dealings, as do Gatsby's links with Wolfshiem, who refuses to get mixed up in Gatsby's affairs now.

This shadowy, crooked figure is counterbalanced by Henry C. Gatz's version of Gatsby, his son Jimmy. Gatz views him as a young, bright man who was sure to make it good.

The **enigmatic quality of Gatsby's character** endures to the novel's end. The reader is left to wonder whether we can ever unravel Gatsby and truly know him. By showing these conflicting versions of the man, the author adds an **air of unreality** to the story, it is difficult to decipher what is real, and who to believe. The **author encourages the reader to revisit Gatsby's superficial life, looking for lasting substance.**

The transient, temporary nature of life is clear as we see how quickly the crowd moves on, and Gatsby is forgotten.

Nick is very thoughtful and reflective as the story closes. The novel's final moments see him bidding farewell to Gatsby's mansion, and considering his friend's hopeful, romantic spirit. There have been moments of loss and regret, but the **lasting impression is one of wonder, and possibility.**

Understanding the Mode
Theme/Issue – Relationships

Relationships has been selected as the theme/issue to explore in this text.
The theme of relationships can be applied to any relationship in a text and includes love, marriage, friendship and family bonds. When analysing this theme consider the complexities of relationships and the impact they have on characters' lives.

Consider the following questions to help you explore the theme of relationships.

- Are relationships generally negative or positive in the text?

- How well do characters communicate and express themselves to one another?

- Do characters trust each other?

- Do characters betray each other?

- Do you see conflict in the relationships in this text?

- Do characters love and respect one another?
  What makes them behave this way?

- How do relationships affect the storyline?

- How are relationships affected by the world of the text?

- Do the relationships in this text make life better or worse for characters?
  Do their relationships bring characters joy or sorrow?

- Are relationships complex and complicated?
  What makes them this way?

- Focus on a single significant relationship in the text – is it positive or negative?
  What makes it this way?

Notes on Theme/Issue - Relationships

Relationships in the novel are complex, rarely being as they seem at first glance. Tom and Daisy, though married to one another, both have **serious, lengthy affairs**, despite remaining committed to one another at the novel's end. **Gatsby's many friends and acquaintances disappear** following his death, suggesting that these **relationships lacked real substance.**

Characters enjoy **romance** in this text - Nick falls in love with Jordan, Tom with Myrtle and Gatsby with Daisy. However, these **romances are temporary and superficial**: Nick tires of Jordan, Tom commits himself to Daisy following Myrtle's death, and Daisy rejects Gatsby in favour of Tom, allowing her lover to take the blame for Myrtle's death while she disappears to safety. In this way, **relationships are seen to be lacking depth and real commitment**, characters change their minds and their hearts with ease. Even Nick's admiration of Gatsby, and his **friendship** with the man, has to be called into question. There are times when Nick has doubts about Gatsby, and the reader has to wonder whether Nick ever knew the real Gatsby at all.

Relationships are characterised by passionate, fleeting emotions. The **male characters in particular are very emotional and feel very strongly**. Gatsby is intent on winning Daisy back after years apart, involving Nick in an elaborate reunion. Tom is similarly impassioned when he undoes Gatsby, fearing he might lose Daisy, and pledges that he will take better care of his wife from now on.

While relationships in the novel are very emotional, many are **damaged** and **lack a grounding in reality**. Just as Gatsby's fantastic parties are exciting and extravagant, and spent by morning, so too are **relationships**

passionate and all-consuming, and quickly over. At one point Nick declares that he is in love with Jordan, but after the car crash, he has little more to do with her.

Fantasy plays a big part in characters' relationships and the way they see themselves. **Gatsby imagines himself married to Daisy, convinced that she never loved her husband.** This of course is not the case, but it is the version of his life he has convinced himself of. His conviction that Daisy must be in love with him highlights how these **relationships are superficially exciting, but deeply flawed.** Characters are in love with the idea of being in love, leading to **emotionally charged, short-lived affairs.**

These **love affairs lead to tensions** between Tom and Gatsby, as both compete for Daisy's heart. This creates a strained atmosphere and uneasiness between them.

It is interesting that **the lasting relationship in the text is that of Tom and Daisy, who have both cheated on each other, and know of the other's infidelity.** Despite their extramarital affairs, they support one another following Myrtle's death and leave town, protecting Daisy from the suspicions of the law.

Nick's romance with Jordan Baker peters out after Myrtle's death. When he realises he has turned thirty and looks to his future, Nick finds Jordan to be a comfort, "the formidable stroke of thirty died away with the reassuring pressure of her hand." However, like the others, **Nick's content is short-lived. His feelings towards Jordan change after the car crash**, and he avoids her, meeting her just once before leaving town.

Friendships in the novel also prove to be false and fleeting. All summer long, Gatsby's mansion overflows with a stream of guests, eager to sample the revelry and luxurious lifestyle on offer. Following Gatsby's death, these 'friends' disappear, as do his business connections, and Nick struggles to find mourners for Gatsby's funeral. These **friendships are non-existent, Gatsby has been used for his wealth.**

Overall, though passionate and exciting, relationships in *The Great Gatsby* **prove to be largely insubstantial and hollow, with few having the strength to last.**

Theme/Issue - Relationships Key Moments

Nick Visits Daisy and Tom

When Nick visits his cousin Daisy and her husband Tom Buchanan, the **complexity and superficiality of their relationships** becomes clear. Nick describes them as **"two old friends whom I scarcely knew at all"**, showing how he is connected to them, but knows very little of them in other ways.

When Tom and Daisy briefly leave, Jordan tells Nick that **Tom has a woman in New York**, something she thought everybody knew. **Tom's infidelity is public knowledge.** There is a **bold, brazen quality to this affair,** as his mistress has just phoned him, making little attempt at secrecy, despite Daisy's presence at home and marriage to Tom.

Tom's affair makes the reader question his commitment to Daisy and scrutinise the nature of their marriage.

While Tom, Daisy and Jordan are happy to see Nick, and chat pleasantly with him, **the reader wonders about the sincerity of their friendship**. It seems they have not been in touch for many years, and now talk of inconsequential things. Nick does not even see Daisy's three year old daughter. The depth of this bond is questionable.

Party in the City

Tom is eager for Nick to meet his mistress and brings him to their apartment in New York to spend an afternoon there. This **openness about his affair** is interesting, he does not seem concerned that Daisy may hear of it. **Tom appears to be completely comfortable with his dual roles of husband and boyfriend.**

The **complexity of Tom's duplicitous relationship** is apparent as the afternoon wears on. Catherine, **Myrtle's sister, claims that neither Tom nor Myrtle can stand the person they are married to**, and that it is Daisy who is blocking their divorce because she is Catholic. Nick knows this to be untrue. It is interesting that **this is the version of Tom's marriage that Catherine is convinced of.**

Myrtle says that marrying her husband was a mistake, suggesting regret over her own situation. However, **Tom himself does not say anything negative about Daisy**, and strikes Myrtle, breaking her nose, when she insists on saying Daisy's name. **This shows that Tom is quick to lash out aggressively at Myrtle. It also shows that Tom values Daisy and holds her in high regard, despite his affair. This episode highlights the complexity of Tom's relationships.**

Gatsby is Reunited with Daisy

Gatsby is nervous and apprehensive on the afternoon he is to meet Daisy, going to great lengths to have everything prepared perfectly. This shows **how important this reunion is to Gatsby**, and how much he wants it to go well.

When they first meet, Daisy and Gatsby are awkward and embarrassed, and Gatsby fears that he has made a terrible mistake. Nick leaves them to become reacquainted and finds them entirely changed when he reappears. Gatsby now radiates wellbeing, while Daisy is full of joy, despite her recent tears. Their relationship has been restored, their romance rekindled.

Aside from their **happiness at being reacquainted**, it is significant to note **Gatsby's desire to show Daisy around his home**. He is thrilled to see her reaction to his extravagant and luxurious possessions. This suggests that **wealth and money influence Gatsby's attractiveness to Daisy**, he is keen for her to realise how rich he is.

Confrontation at the Plaza Hotel

The question of Gatsby and Daisy's relationship is resolved in the Plaza Hotel, following a challenge from Tom.

Tom accuses Gatsby of causing trouble in his house, before shredding Gatsby's reputation and **affirming his commitment to Daisy**. **Tom downplays his affairs as minor indiscretions**, calling them "sprees", and claims that **he loves Daisy all the while. He admits to being unfaithful, but is determined not to lose his wife, asserting that they are staying together.**

Gatsby is severely affected by the idea that Daisy loved Tom as well as him. This shows **Gatsby's idealised, romantic idea of love. He cannot accept that Daisy ever loved another as much as she loves him.**

Tom successfully wins back Daisy in this scene, belittling Gatsby and reducing him to a bootlegger in Daisy's eyes. Tom is so confident that their affair is over that he sends them home together, in Gatsby's car. **Tom successfully takes on, and defeats his love rival, preserving his marriage.**

Post Accident

Tom is shocked to discover that Myrtle has been killed in a hit and run. However, he is quick to tell Wilson to pull himself together, and deny ownership of the yellow car Wilson saw him in that afternoon. **Despite the shock of Myrtle's death, Tom is calculating and shrewd in his actions, protecting himself from being linked to the accident.**

Leaving the scene, Tom accelerates and **breaks down in tears, clearly moved and upset by Myrtle's death** and his belief that Gatsby didn't even stop his car after hitting her. This shows that **Tom felt strongly about Myrtle, their relationship meant something to him.**

Gatsby's only concern after the accident is how Daisy is doing. **He intends to say he was driving and bear full responsibility for Myrtle's death**, even though Daisy was driving the car when it killed her. Gatsby even **stands vigil** outside her house in case Tom bothers her after the argument in the Plaza Hotel that afternoon. **Gatsby is entirely devoted to Daisy here, his feelings are steadfast, if misplaced**, after the afternoon's events.

When Nick looks in the pantry window of Tom and Daisy's he sees them sitting together, talking closely. Nick notes the **natural intimacy** of the scene, as if they are **conspiring together.** It appears that **Tom and Daisy's relationship, despite the day's troubling events, is very solid and secure**.

The moments following the crash make clear how passionately Tom felt about Myrtle, but also how determined he is to save Daisy.

Gatsby remains devoted to Daisy, he does not consider how his relationship with her has changed, or the strength of her bond with Tom.

Nick's Loyalty to Gatsby After His Death

The final chapter charts events after Gatsby's murder. As his neighbour's friends disappear and fail to honour his memory, **Nick emerges as a devoted friend to Gatsby.**

Nick attempts to raise mourners for the funeral and put Gatsby's affairs in order as best he can. He feels a sense of responsibility to him, and cannot abandon him now that he is dead.

When Gatsby's father asks, **Nick says they were close friends; he is not ashamed of his friendship with Gatsby like some. Loyalty and friendship characterise this relationship**, Nick genuinely feels for his friend.

Nick describes the East as being haunted for him after Gatsby's death, and he decides to go back home. **Nick has been changed by his relationship with Gatsby**, a truth that he is not afraid to acknowledge. Nick's **steadfast friendship and devotion to Gatsby** is highlighted as it contrasts so sharply with the willingness of others to forget him and disown any connections they may have had. **Although Nick never really knew Gatsby, he valued him, and continues to do so after his death.**

Understanding the Mode
Hero, Heroine, Villain
(Ordinary Level)

'Hero, Heroine, Villain' refers to studying central characters (protagonists/antagonists).
Their traits, values, etc. and their ability to deal with conflict, challenges, obstacles, etc. should be considered.
Think about a character's personality, their behaviour, what you like and dislike about them, etc.

Focus on a single character as you consider the following questions:

- Is this character a 'good' main character?
  Are they interesting?
  Are they likeable?
  Do you care about what happens to them? Why/why not?

- What problems and difficulties do they face?
  Do they find facing these problems easy?

- What does this character struggle with?

- What are they good at?

- What makes this character happy?

- Do you feel sorry for this character at any point? Why/why not?

- What sort of life has this character had?
  How has this affected them?

- Describe this character's personality.

- What is important to this character?

- If you had a conversation with this character, what would you talk about?
  What advice would you offer them?
  Do you think they would be an easy person to talk to about their problems? Why/why not?

- Do you like this character?
  What makes you feel this way?

Notes on Hero, Heroine, Villain (Ordinary Level)

Jay Gatsby is a mystery. He is an enigmatic man, difficult to figure out as **so much about him is unknown**. Fantastic rumours and gossip surround him, adding to his air of mystery and celebrity.

His fantastic, lavish parties demonstrate his **wealth and generosity**. This also feeds into our impression of this rich man, who falls **hopelessly in** love with Nick's cousin, Daisy.

Gatsby created his identity at seventeen, inventing Jay Gatsby out of James Gatz. He **served in the army, attended Oxford** for a time, and is now **extremely wealthy,** though **the source of his income is criminal** according to Tom Buchanan.

It is impossible to truly know Gatsby. He lies to Nick about his family dying and inheriting their fortune, but we later meet his father, Mr Gatz, at Gatsby's funeral. He also lies about his business connections, trying to conceal the illegal aspects of his business.

He is also very romantic and committed, steadfast in his love of Daisy, even after the car crash. His romantic side suggests a naivity or vulnerability about him, he believes entirely in fairytale love stories and happy endings, where he and Daisy will be together after so many years apart.

It is **after Gatsby's death that the reader must wonder how well we knew the real Gatsby.** His friends and acquaintances disappear, and the few connections that Nick can make contact with seem suspicious. **Once he has died, his persona begins to unravel, and Gatsby the lavish host and generous near-celebrity vanishes into thin air.**

We never really know Gatsby. As the story ends he remains something of a mystery, a man of many parts, part rich host, part gangster, part victim of Wilson's jealousy.

Gatsby's death results from mistaken identity, an ironic fact for a man with so many different selves.

Hero, Heroine, Villain Key Moments

Gatsby's Reputation

Gatsby's reputation precedes him. Nick **hears about his rich, glamorous neighbour before he ever meets him**, and sees firsthand **the stream of guests, servants and elaborate preparations that go into Gatsby's extravagant parties**, "There was music from my neighbour's house through the summer nights."

Nick is invited to one of Gatsby's parties and is eager to meet him, "but the two or three people of whom I asked his whereabouts stared at me in… an amazed way." Gatsby, it seems, is difficult to pin down.

Rumours abound about Gatsby, the **guests at Gatsby's party are full of gossip about him**, saying he killed a man, and that he was a German spy during the war. He is a man of **mystery, glamour** and excitement, who can never free himself from gossip, speculation and suspicion.

Lunch in the City with Nick

Gatsby takes Nick to lunch in the city to get to know him better, as he wants Nick to do a favour for him. Gatsby is **keen to give Nick a good impression of who he is**, rather than Nick basing his view of him on stories that he hears. There is something **old-fashioned and formal** in this, that Gatsby feels the need to explain who he is before he asks Nick for help.

Gatsby says that Jordan will speak to Nick about this matter (which turns out to be arranging a meeting with Daisy). **Gatsby wants Daisy to see his house, keen to impress her with his wealth and beautiful home**), which adds to the impression of him as formal and conservative.

Gatsby chooses the parts of his past to represent to Nick. Gatsby speaks about inheriting his wealth, the war, and his time at Oxford amongst other things. He produces a military medal and a photograph from Oxford, proving his past. **Nick is not entirely sure that he believes his story**, wondering if Gatsby is pulling his leg. Gatsby chooses these aspects of his past to discuss with Nick, **hoping to make a good impression** so that Nick will help him.

At lunch, Nick meets Wolfshiem, Gatsby's friend and business connection. **Wolshiem is a gambler, involved in shady business dealings, and he adds another dimension to our view of Gatsby**. The reader is forced to consider what we really know about Gatsby, and **who he really is**.

The lunch ends when Nick sees Tom Buchanan and goes to introduce Gatsby to him, only to discover that Gatsby has left. This lunch episode shows that he is an **intriguing character**, with **many aspects to his past and character**.

Meeting Daisy

Gatsby's meeting with Daisy shows his **romantic, hopeful** side and his devotion to the idea of love. **Gatsby makes a great effort to have everything arranged for his meeting with Daisy**. He wears a splendid suit, and has Nick's house decorated with flowers and the lawn cut beforehand. He is **anxious that this meeting should go well** between them, but is nervous and embarrassed when Daisy first arrives. This may suggest how much he wants things to go well.

Nick leaves them alone and returns a short while later, to find Gatsby glowing. **Rekindling his relationship with Daisy makes him enormously happy.**

Gatsby invites Daisy and Nick to come and look around his home. **He wishes to impress Daisy with his incredible wealth and beautiful mansion.** This shows the **importance of money to Gatsby**. He feels **it makes him a more impressive, attractive man.**

Tom Ends Gatsby's Affair with Daisy

On the afternoon of the showdown with Tom in the Plaza Hotel, Gatsby and Daisy kiss passionately when Tom leaves the room. However, despite the seriousness of their affair, **Gatsby avoids speaking to Tom about his relationship with Daisy**, telling Nick he **cannot say anything in Tom's house**. This shows his **formal, conservative nature**.

Later, in the Plaza Hotel, Tom interrogates Gatsby about his past. Gatsby responds by telling Tom that Daisy is in love with him, and that she never loved Tom. For Gatsby, this is very significant, **he believes that his relationship with Daisy is unique and incomparable to her marriage.** He has a very **romantic, idealistic view of his relationship with Daisy**, and he cannot accept that she also loved Tom.

Gatsby tells Tom that Daisy is leaving him, an intention that crumbles when Tom reveals that Gatsby is involved in selling grain alcohol over the counter in his drug-stores. **Tom adds that Gatsby has something even bigger going on now, ruining him in Daisy's eyes.** Gatsby shied away from this conflict with Tom, and now Tom undoes him. In this scene **Gatsby's romantic hopes are dashed by Tom's knowledge of his illegal activities and suspicious business dealings.**

Attempting to Protect Daisy After the Accident

After the car crash, Gatsby remains devoted to Daisy, despite the events in the Plaza Hotel, where Tom revealed Gatsby was a crook and quashed Daisy's affair with him. **Gatsby however, does not accept that things with Daisy are over, believing that she loves him**. He stands outside her home in a **pathetic vigil**, in case Tom should bother her. **He shows an innocence and naivity in his inability to realise that Tom and Daisy will stay together**, and do all they can to keep Daisy out of the matter of Myrtle's death.

Gatsby intends to take the blame for the crash, and say that he was driving, "of course I'll say I was." **He thinks he can protect Daisy and is willing to sacrifice himself to do so, casting him in a romantic light.**

Post Death Version of Gatsby

Our understanding of Gatsby's character does not end with his death, but continues to develop right up until the story's end.

Nick speaks of nightmare stories in the press covering Gatsby's death, and says "**I found myself on Gatsby's side, and alone.**" **Now that he is dead, Gatsby's friends and acquaintances have disappeared**. Daisy and Tom have left town and Meyer Wolfshiem declines to attend the funeral.

In the midst of this, Nick finds himself involved in dealings he does not fully understand, answering a phonecall from Chicago to hear that young Parke has been picked up. The call disconnects when Nick says that Gatsby is dead, adding to the **mystery around Gatsby's business affairs**.

Gatsby's father, Henry C. Gatz, comes from Minnesota. **He refers to**

his son as "Jimmy", adding to the sense that we never knew who the real Gatsby was. Gatsby's artificial life of wealth, popularity and glamour ends with his death, showing how insubstantial his persona really was. **He is buried virtually friendless, with his social circle keen to forget him.**

www.ingramcontent.com/pod-product-compliance
Lightning Source LLC
Chambersburg PA
CBHW071039080526
44587CB00015B/2689